RUBANK

SOLO AND ENSEMBLE SERIES

EMMETT'S LULLABY

TRANS. G.E. HOLMES

for BB♭ BASS (TUBA)
with piano accompaniment

Featured by William Bell, Bass Soloist with Armco Band and Cincinnati Symphony Orchestra.

EMMETT'S LULLABY

TRANSCRIPTION

BB♭ BASS
(SOUSAPHONE)

G.E. HOLMES

Also published with Band Acc.

EMMETT'S LULLABY

TRANSCRIPTION

PIANO ACC.

Solo for BB♭ Bass

G. E. HOLMES

Andante moderato
f
rall.
p
a little faster
slight rit.
a tempo
rall.
L.H.
R.H.
R.H.
L.H.
daintily
slower

rit.
R. H.
rit.
Tutti
f
VAR. I
mp

rall.
a tempo
rall.
accel.
a tempo
slower
slower
Tutti
f
VAR II.
mp
mp

rall.
accel.
rall.
accel.
a tempo
a tempo
slower
3
3
3
3
slower

Tutti
Cad.
slow
slow accel.
Vivace
mf
mf
ff
ff

rall.
accel.
a tempo
Slower
Tutti
f
Var. II
mp
rall.
accel.
a tempo
Slower
Tutti
f
rall.
slow
Cadenza
slow
accel.
Vivace
mf
ff

TUBA SOLOS with Piano Accompaniment

HL04479309	Asleep in the Deep (Petrie/arr. Walters) *Grade 2.5*
HL04479310	Auld Lang Syne (Air and Variations) (DeLamater) *Grade 2.5*
HL04479313	Bombastoso (Caprice) (VanderCook) *Grade 2.5*
HL04479314	Carnival of Venice – Fantasia (Holmes) *Grade 4*
HL04479317	Colossus (Air and Variations) (VanderCook) *Grade 3*
HL04479318	Concertante (Walters) *Grade 4*
HL04479319	Concertpiece (Painparé/rev. H. Voxman) *Grade 4.5*
HL04479321	Emmett's Lullaby (trans. Holmes) *Grade 4*
HL04479322	Forty Fathoms (Walters) *Grade 2.5*
HL04479323	In the Hall of the Mountain King (Grieg/arr. Holmes) *Grade 2*
HL04479324	The Jolly Peasant (Fantasy) (Schumann/arr. Holmes) *Grade 2.5*
HL04479327	March of a Marionette (Gounod/arr. Walters) *Grade 2.5*
HL04479330	Rocked in the Cradle of the Deep (Air and Variations) (DeLamater) *Grade 3*

BRASS ENSEMBLES

Instrumentation as marked

HL04479733	Aria and Minuet (brass quintet; alt. parts included) (Scarlatti/arr. Johnson) *Grade 3*
HL04479744	Chorale and March (two trumpets, horn, trombone, baritone B.C., tuba) (Beethoven/arr. Lotzenhiser) *Grade 3*
HL04479714	Donnybrook (four trombones *or* two trombones, baritone, tuba) (Ostransky) *Grade 2*
HL04479746	Four Chorales for Brass Sextet (Bach/arr. Johnson) *Grade 2*
HL04479736	If Thou Be Near (brass quintet; alt. parts included) (Bach/arr. Beeler) *Grade 3*
HL04479719	March of a Marionette (four trombones *or* two trombones, baritone, tuba) (Gounod/arr. Lotzenhiser) *Grade 3*
HL04479738	Quintet in B Minor – Third Movement (brass quintet; alt. parts included) (Ewald/ed.Voxman) *Grade 5*
HL04479741	Sonata No. 27 (brass quintet; alt. parts included) (Pezel/arr. Brown) *Grade 2*
HL04479863	Spanish Dance No. 4 (brass sextet or choir) (Moszkowski/arr. Holmes) *Grade 4*
HL04479749	Suite for Brass Sextet (two trumpets, horn, trombone, baritone B.C., tuba) (Ostransky) *Grade 3*
HL04479752	Trumpet Tune and Air (two trumpets, horn, trombone, baritone B.C., tuba) (Purcell/arr. Brown) *Grade 2*
HL04479723	Two Episodes (four trombones *or* two trombones, baritone, tuba) (Ostransky) *Grade 2*
HL04479859	Two Intradas (two trumpets, horn, trombone, baritone B.C., tuba) (Franck/trans. Long) *Grade 2*
HL04479860	Woodland Sketches (brass sextet or choir) (MacDowell/arr. Johnson) *Grade 2*

U.S. $7.99

HL04479321